Body Beautiful

Ifor Thomas was born in Pembrokeshire. He was a founder member of *Cabaret 246*, *Horses' Mouth* and *Working Title Writers* – all performance-based writing groups, and has tutored poetry in performance at Arvon, Totleigh Barton and Ty Newydd. He has performed at festivals throughout the UK and in venues as diverse as the Tunnel Club in London to the Millennium Centre Cardiff. He has won the John Tripp award for spoken poetry and been a prize winner in the Cardiff International poetry competition. His poems have been widely published and anthologised. His last collection, *Unsafe Sex* is also published by Parthian.

Body Beautiful

Ifor Thomas

Parthian
The Old Surgery
Napier Street
Cardigan
SA43 1ED

www.parthianbooks.co.uk

First published in 2005
Reprinted 2006
© Ifor Thomas 2005
All Rights Reserved

ISBN 1-902638-61-1
       9 781902 638614

Editor: Richard Gwyn
Cover design by Lucy Llewellyn
Printed and bound by Dinefwr Press, Llandybïe, Wales
Typeset by type@lloydrobson.com

Published with the financial support of the Welsh
Books Council.

British Library Cataloguing in Publication Data

A cataloguing record for this book is available from the
British Library

Acknowledgements

Some poems in this collection have previously appeared in *New Welsh Review*, *Poetry Wales*, *Yellow Crane* and in anthologies from Rattapallax, Red Poets' Society and Seren.

Contents

For Gill

My recurring nightmare is trigonometry

Once again I am sitting at a small desk
the single unblinking eye of a blank inkwell,
old wood as hard and polished as stone
cratered with carving, unknown initials.

My pens and pencils, a rubber, set square
are marshalled like troops deployed to the wrong front.
The examination paper is virgin snow,
tracked only by wild animals.

An invigilator patrols the varnished straits,
the breath of his gown on my cheek,
heels clicking, out of time with the clock
whose ornate hands do not move.

Exam panic grips my throat, sweats my hand –
why am I doing the trigonometry paper?

> *I am fifty-five;*
> *I own my house, car.*
> *My children are gone.*
> *I run my business.*
> *My marriage is secure.*

But still the trigonometry question demands an answer.

New questions

Sister Vivienne, Researcher,
shows me the medical illustration –
it's as foreign as a map of Glasgow or Leeds.
She tests my knowledge.
I know all this but not now.
This isn't my city.
I'm lost.

She tells me how difficult diagnosis is,
how imponderable treatment.
There are forms to sign,
questionnaires to complete,
consents and blood to be given.
Do I understand?
Will I participate?

We sit together alone in the
disused hospital. This was once
the A&E department.
I came here with my children,
their cuts and broken bones
were tended in a cubicle such as this.
I remember a nurse, his name was Mal.

I puzzle over this theme park –
bladder like a boating lake,
the sweeping cycle path of the urethra
the country lane of the rectum
the race track of the penis
the car park of the prostate –
like all car parks, it's difficult to get to.

For a moment I am glad
that these things are foreign to me –
that I am not an expert,
that all this is unexplored territory.

When I am chemo-whacked
and zapped by X-rays
I will know these byways
like the IV-stabbed back of my hand,
will have conducted guided tours,
allowed visitors
memorabilia and takeaways.

Then my grey-skinned face
will nod the answers to her questions.

Llawhaden: 19 May 2000

Edith Thomas, 91, lies lost in the rubble
of C16 Llawhaden House. She has stumbled
once too often, this time into the two bar electric fire
and her nightie has turned her into a roman candle.

Johnny Owen, 89, the last man to see her alive,
after 68 years now unemployed, says, '*she was a real lady.*'
PC Cowper, 25, drapes the scene-of-crime tape.
He is a police officer destined for a good career.

Opposite Llawhaden House is Llawhaden Castle
built by Bernard, the first Norman bishop of St. David's.
Llawhaden straddles the Landsker, both English and Welsh
were once spoken here. The fire fighters all speak English.

My mother, 85, fluently bilingual, fiercely Welsh,
peers through the Herris fencing for an interesting cutting,
opts instead for a 2-inch screw dropped by the builder
who erected the DANGER DO NOT ENTER sign.

This visit pleases my mother, scathing as she is of
                            old women who live alone,
drowning in their baths, burning down their mansions,
going ga-ga without style or presence of mind
while she sails on serenely.

Home visit

The chapel by the roadside
was built where a preacher
delivered his sermon.

Gravestones stand
in vague rows, some leaning
as if trying to hear his words
over time and traffic.

I drive by, travelling to see my mother
who waits, wrapped in old age,
to tell me again stories
that I do not listen to
as I clear past-its-sell-by-date, half-eaten food
out of her refrigerator.

It is only when I drive away
that I think of that time
when I will strain
to hear her voice,
shifting, fading.

The lie of the land

I'm not like these
old men in the waiting room
with dyed hair,
white hair, worried look
in their eyes.
I'm tanned, lean,
fitter than I've been
for a long while.

> *Ah*, says Sister Vivienne
> *this cancer*
> *sneaks up on you,*
> *you can be feeling good*
> *until the day you die.*
> *On the other hand...*

(the consultant
has his
up my rectum
he's checking
the lie of the land).

Sgwd yr eira

Skull tested to concussion
cords of cold plait my intestines
currents I can stand on
suddenly collapse.

In the sack
of this carcase

the worm is turning.

I drive my car thinking

I am expecting the worst so
I drive my car thinking
what it's like to be dead.

When he says that
3 out of the 10 biopsy
sites show cancer,
it is almost good news.
There will be an MRI,
bone scan.

I phone my friend –
he's done this,
gone back to work
within 3 weeks.
He says it's OK,
he's got control of his bladder.

I ask what his sex life is like.
Was better
he replies.

I drive my car thinking.

Sitting tight

I thought death
was something that happened
to other people –
AIDS-ravaged Africans
dying like there's no tomorrow,
sad old saps in
the EMI ward,
crated up and carted off
on a daily basis
or even the boy hit by a van
on Lake Road East
whose flowers still adorn
the tree that marks the spot.

Me?
My destiny is to observe,
until the end of time,
scarfed in my white beard,
wise and lonely
but alive.

Now, like a weather vane,
the finger has swung round
and is pointing in my direction.
An x-ray result will settle the score
mark me down for a last
world trip or whatever else

you do when eternity
is reduced to seeing out November
or maybe December.

Nothing to do but sit tight,
hope the wind will change.

Kiss

I knew something was wrong
when I kissed you that afternoon,
not the coldness of your forehead – we all get cold,
nor its smoothness – your skin was always good.

It was, I think, the fact that you let me kiss you at all.
You always turned away from such shows of affection.

Death has certainly changed you.

MRI

I lie face up on the trolley
blanket covering my bare legs,
plastic board placed over my groin.
There is a single thin pillow,
my ears are plugged.
The trolley is raised
and I am offered up to the machine.

It devours me
in bite-sized chunks.
I slip into its smooth gullet.
It chunters and groans
stops, rests, starts again.

I think of small creatures trapped in
microwave ovens.

They asked me if I had:

> *A cardiac pacemaker*
> *A cochlear implant*
> *A spinal chord stimulator*
> *An artificial heart valve*
> *An intracranial aneurysm clip*

And

> *Metal fragments in my eye*

Now totally absorbed into its plastic gut
I think
> *What if I do have a metal fragment in my eye?*

A remnant of a long-ago car crash
a childish accident,
something I have forgotten or
don't even know about.

There is a rubber bulb in my hand
they said to squeeze it will stop the machine.
But I know different:
it squirts water
through a plastic flower
placed on the nurse's tunic
and believe me
if my eyes are sucked out by this monster
somebody will get a drenching.

Rust

In October the colour of my sperm
changed to rust.
In tune with the changing season
but frightening the shit
out of me and Gill as we lay,
post-coital, staring at the ceiling.

Scribbles

I tell her to spin the wheel
or, in this case, phone a computer in Bristol.
I've got three choices
surgery, watchful waiting, x-rays.

There's a pause:
our eyes meet and I think
I detect sympathy
then she looks to her notepad,
scribbles a flower.
It's only her job after all.

I hear connections being made.
The line of her lips tightens.
I look closer at her note pad:
it's not a flower
but a lucky four leaf clover.

Cut, keep or cook

They don't know what to do
About prostate cancer
So they leave it to you
To come up with the answer.

There's a computer, or formbook,
That will randomly choose
Whether to cut, keep or cook.
Heads they win, tails you lose.

The net

It's all there on the net –
the medical sites, chatrooms,
the stories of those who lived,
who died, who survived
against the odds.

A mouse button rolls
and the screen flickers
in the eyes of another
hopeful traveller of this virtual
theme park of freaks,
heroes and fantasists.

> *Since 1950 $200 billion*
> *has been spent on cancer research*
> *yet the death rates from cancer*
> *are the same as in 1950.*
>
> *'Drinking diesel killed my cancer . . .'*
>
> *'I grew a new set of lungs...'*
>
> *What are the rates of survival*
> *of testicular cancer?*
>
> *testicular cancer followed by prostate cancer?*
>
> *death?*

I switch off the monitor,
retrieve the crumpled paper –

'report for pre-operative check-up 26 January
admission on Wednesday, op on Thursday...'

no stats, no stories.

Reality slips through the net.

Smile

Now your account is closed.
Your trip to the furnace is signalled
by the whirr of curtains
that consign you from view.

As the words of the Welsh hymn
climb into the air of the crematorium
the sentiment of Reverend Thomas,
like embalming fluid, seeps into our sadness.

If corpses can have a last smile
then I guess your lips twitched
because all in all it went well.
No protracted goodbyes, you hated those.

No being waited on, I never even
made you a cup of tea.
You outlasted your brother and sister
and chose to die when Mrs L was on holiday –

didn't want her having the satisfaction
of sniffing into her hanky saying
sad so sad – we'll all miss her so.
No, that would have marred the day.

I wish I'd been with you
when you drank the cup of water,
before the sudden pain in your chest
rose up and pulled you to the floor.

The last eyes you looked into
were those of the cat
suspicious of this new game
which involved you hogging the carpet.

But then again, as you said often enough,
some things are best done alone.
The Reverend has finished,
a jay flies across the garden as we leave.

Hotel Rossiya – in memoriam

My ghost has a good choice –
three thousand rooms and some to spare,
a shuffle across from Red Square.

I never felt at home in the mausoleum –
Lenin, pickled in pride and formaldehyde
Being no company for this fun-lovin' Georgian.

Even so, for that jumped-up clown
Who backed down when the going got tough
To dump my corpse under the wall, was a bit much.

Now I sometimes take a beer
In the south entrance of the Hotel Rossiya
Though it's hard to catch the eye

Of the girls behind the bar
They get bigger tips from the tourists.
I don't feel as if I'm made of steel, these days.

I met a football supporter from Wales
Who couldn't believe how much I've aged.
We both could smile looking back now.

The Rhondda was part of the USSR
I said. Except for the gulags, he replied.
I waved that carping criticism aside.

Look at Solzhenitsyn, did wonders for his career!
We got on well and I fixed the result.
A bit of a bore, Russia/Wales a 0-0 draw.

Now I hear these guys from the Duma
Have agreed with Putin that the hotel
Is too reminiscent of the 'old days' –

Pah! somebody's made an estimate
There is too much value in the real estate
For even a nod to history –

Biggest hotel in the world, socialist leaning,
first to introduce central vacuum cleaning.
Six thousand souls crated in peace

The very model of a society at ease,
Even if the paperwork is onerous.
Now the world's moved on, harder to please.

There's no place I can call heaven.
Even the Welshman had a mobile
Said he'd text me from Blaenavon.

Moscow is not the place I knew.
My ghost will rest with my bones
Under the Kremlin's foundation stones.

Pre-op day

This is like a school fete
Where you have to visit all the stalls.

You give urine in Suite 18
Before heading off on a treasure trail

Which involves blood samples,
Electro cardiograph, blood oxygen, blood pressure.

I team up with a joiner from Merthyr
Who's done all this before and knows the tricks –

For instance, blood samples is popular
So go and get your queue ticket,

But don't wait, go to ECG
And hope you haven't lost your place.

It works, nobody is waiting at ECG.
She tapes electrodes and runs the chart in minutes.

Back at blood samples we are up the queue –
He's getting remedial work after a wrecked urethra

But that was in Prince Charles
And we are in the Heath.

I return to my starting point.
Last thing is blood pressure.

She says BP is good
112 over 57

I should survive.
But, she warns, nothing is certain in surgery.

Which reminds me –
I still have to visit the raffle ticket stall.

The hospital

In the early morning
the hospital is a nuclear reactor.
Square, massive, it looms over
Heath Park as silent as Chernobyl.

The grass is crisp from frost.
My breath comes in rhythmic gasps.
I do the runner's checks –
muscles, joints, lungs, heart.

I've trained for this
as athletes do for the big race,
visualise victory, remove negativity –
run through, not to, the finish.

I've stood before a mirror,
felt the razor shave my gut –
seen the surgeon's blade
draw that first line of red.

But then it goes dark.
(How could I have foreseen
The cannula, drip, wound drains
catheter bag, the sound of death in the next bed?)

I quicken my pace.
The force field of the hospital
is drawing me in.

Nightshirt

I walk into the 9-bed ward.
I've got an overnight bag.
My bed is against the wall
opposite the door,
not quite in pole position
but good enough.

I walk around in my jeans,
Introduce myself
to Bill, from the Heath,
Ron, from Cathays,
John (Ely)
and Phil, somewhere in dementia.

They don't talk much –
not until I don my nightshirt,
become one of them.

The score

The consultant arrives with his retinue –
Registrar, Mr Brown; staff nurse Jane;
others, whose functions are not clear.

He tells me –
prostate, lymph glands,
seminal vessel, left-side nerve bundle,
all to be removed.

He says I've got a Gleeson score of 7.
Is that bad? I query.
It's worse than 6, he replies.

The retinue stares.
No sympathy –
just the thrill of the chase.

Poleaxed

Even the registrar speaks in awe
of the laxative – poleaxe.
Hours later, after two sachets,
I've pebble-dashed the
WC pan and I'm still making a run
for the bog at midnight.
My mobile drip stand
rattles over the ward floor,
jams in the cubicle door,
arm extended.
I drop just in time.

I study the indentations in the vinyl
while my arse gasps like a stranded fish.

I return across the darkened ward:
the grunts, coughs and farts
sound as if I'm billeted on
an active volcano.

My drip stand,
in supermarket trolley fashion,
skitters around so I'm forced to dance,
bare feet skipping clear of the spinning wheels.

Snow

The metal window frame,
single sheet of glass,
offer little against the storm.
My face feels the draught.

I grip the cill, look down
from the fifth floor, watch snow
swirl around the lights
at the hospital entrance.

A man exits bending against the wind
into the orange glow,
a plastic bag clutched to his chest.
like a buoyancy aid.

If I were to reach out
and catch a spinning snowflake
it would dissolve on first touch
leaving not even the wetness of a kiss.

The snow blurs edges,
puts down a carpet of silence
as if royalty were in residence
and did not want to be disturbed.

Not royalty, but the dignitaries
of disease, dying, trauma
in theatre gowns, wearing cannulas,
carrying fluid bags, rattling drip stands

travel long corridors
mumbling medical monologues.
Patients in this 9-bed ward
ponder their fleeting preoccupations.

I stand at the window
facing the immensity of night,
feeling the breeze burn my cheek.

Breached

The nurse from Zambia
wakens me at six, says
wash, put on the theatre gown
soon they will take you down.

Water runs over my
soon-to-be scarred skin.
I stand in the shower,
notice how fear tastes sour.

I refuse general anaesthetic
opting to stay awake.
There's a paper screen between
me and the cutting scene.

I think of a magician
sawing his assistant in half;
there's no blood, no gore, so neat –
smiling head next to the soles of her feet.

With morphine induced bonhomie
I definitely can't feel pain
it's more like the surgeon's washing dishes
in my body's deep recesses.

I don't know where
I stop and the outside begins –
I'm breached, blurred, worn thin.
Is this where dying seeps in?

Anaesthetic room

I arrive in the anaesthetic room.
A new cannula is fixed.
I arch my back.
A nurse holds my hand as
the injection is administered
into my spine.

In front of me the theatre doors
swing open.

Masked men and women in blue,
students in a line,
drip stands, theatre lights, paper screen,
rows of instruments around the
operating table.

The doors shut.
I lie down.
Waiting for the anaesthetic to kick in
I think of Timothy McVeigh.

The second hand sweeps round.
Is now the right time
to tell them
I've changed my mind?

Mid-surgery

It appears around the screen in a jar:
gobbet red with that tinge of brown
sometimes seen on fillet steak.
No sign of tumours, cells in revolt.

I condemn it to dissection, pickling,
to be sectioned in slides,
gawped at by students with hangovers.

My curse is formaldehyde.

Blocking signals to the heart

Timothy McVeigh's last meal was
two pints of mint choc chip ice cream.
Out of character this, if, as reported,
he had adopted a strict vegan diet
to encourage the gaunt look of a martyr.
Still he keeps us guessing.
There is a small delay in the execution chamber –
problems with the live CCTV feed to Oklahoma.
The ten media representatives are patient
(as well they may be – this is a once-in-a-career opportunity).

>   *Sodium pentathol is an anaesthetic*
>   *It stops the brain reacting to nervous impulses.*

He keeps his eyes open – they all agree on this
but does he lift his head from the gurney
to stare defiantly at those who stare at him?
Not certain. The IV was already fixed to his right thigh
ready to deliver the three chemical cocktail.
A sheet covers his body and is folded over his chest
we must see his face as he dies
(unusual this, in most pornographic movies
the face is the last thing we want to see).
The IV line jumps as the chemicals flow.

>   *Pancuronium bromide, is related to curare,*
>   *It paralyses the breathing muscles.*

He is now staring at the camera in the ceiling,
(our eye witness has it that he does not blink).
He takes puffs of air *as if fighting unconsciousness*
(so he is defiant!)
After four minutes his eyes
glaze over, roll up slightly,
his skin turns yellow
his lips tinged blue.

Potassium chloride blocks electrical signals to the heart.

Nil By

I am gutted, morphine fluff tickling my nose,
IV in, wounds draining and catheter bag urine
blobbing with blood. Welcome back to the ward.

Snores, grunts and farts rumble and flow.
The monitor over the empty bed in the far corner
glows blue as veins, dawn is worryingly grey-faced.

In another hour the nurses will break open this tomb
of the living dead and those that can walk will
stagger like zombies into the morning.

Thermometers will probe our ears,
BP monitors, blood oxygen clips, will search for signs
of life in the ruins of our carcases.

For the survivors there will be Weetabix
toast and jam dispensed by the fat man,
who addresses everyone by their names

Except me, known as Nil By these last two days.
My teeth crush the contraband segment of grapefruit;
juice flows down my throat like mercury.

Body Beautiful

I wear my jewellery –
A cannula on the back of each wrist.

My bodily adornments –
Wound drains, catheter.

My piercings –
A suture through the foreskin, staples.

My tattoo –
A six-inch scar.

In urology
I'm dressed to kill.

Gutted

Telling me of her home, she says *gutted*
in a soft Zambian voice, lips so close
I can feel her breath.

I forget that
she is a nurse,
and I her patient.

The *English Fish* – so called
as a joke on the explorers who said
they had discovered it,

is best simply gutted and baked.
Her touch lingers
but her eyes remember

a freshwater lake near her village
where fishermen hang nets in
the sun and one, who carries

the memory of her skin
as the glitter of fish scales
on his fingers.

Rev mo

Her hand
knuckles my stomach,
grasps the wound drain.

I see Sharkey's work-stained fist,
right hand holding the rope
left flat on the outboard engine.

His arm jerks back,
a punch in reverse motion.
The engine splutters.

Perhaps seeing him
led me to here
living his cancer in rev mo.

Her nurse's fist pulls,
uncoiling that starting rope
spinning out of my guts.

Roger Pleace

Roger Pleace walks
on the balls of his
bare feet. In 1957
the heavyweight champion of Wales.
He was never knocked down.

Even now, in pyjamas,
this boilermaker
from Grangetown
looks hard to beat.

Two weeks he's been here
wondering where
the next punch is coming from.

Bill Tarrant

Bill Tarrant wakes at 7.30am
is helped from his bed.
Sits next to it until
he is helped back in at 9.30pm.

Bill is 93 and speaks quietly
so that you have to lean
to catch his words.
He introduces himself to strangers:

> *My name is Bill Tarrant*
> *I was born in 1911*
> *I wanted to be a surgeon*
> *But my father wouldn't let me*
> *I volunteered for the RAF*
> *And went to Africa.*

We celebrate the arrival of his new bed:
motorised, it can adopt an infinite number of positions.
Now he doesn't even have to get up.

That night, in the early hours
a voice rings out; loud, clear,

> *MY NAME IS BILL TARRANT*
> *I WAS BORN IN 1911*
> *AND THIS IS THE WORST BED*
> *I HAVE EVER SLEPT IN.*

New bed

Ron and I stand next to Bill
who lies in his new bed.
It cost the NHS ten grand.

How's the bed, Bill?
Ron is the MC of the ward
and is genial to everyone
even the boorish knight
in the corner cubicle.

Fine says Bill.
He has the patience of old age
having cared for his sick wife
for twenty years.

It's electric Bill – you could drive it to London.
No point, says Ron, *nowhere to park.*
Bill stares back from behind his beard,
wonders what brought him to this.

Pill round

Before lights out at 10.30
there is the pill round.
Sleeping pills, laxatives, pain killers –
you can have what you want.

Bill has a new bed
and is comfortably asleep
long before Daisy arrives
pushing the pill trolley.

She has to shake him awake:
sleepy, confused and deaf
she shouts the choices.
He yawns, blinks

asks for a sleeping pill.

Breakfast

Bruce cracks the same joke every morning.
When asked whether he wants

> *weetabix, corn flakes, porridge*
> *brown toast, white toast,*
> *marge, butter,*
> *jam, marmalade, marmite*
> *tea, coffee?*

He replies *yes*
then laughs insanely.
Bill on the other hand
always says *pardon?*

The knight in the corner cubicle

He fends off nurses
frightens fellow patients
is generally disagreeable.

Sir Galahad is unhorsed
the queen's colours
hang bedraggled from his broken lance.

He roars and grunts
securing his castle by
drawing the cubicle curtains.

He rests on his shield
a warrior between wars
weary but unbowed.

The next day the torturers arrive
wheel him off to the dungeons
crack his bones, scour his skin

pour hot oil into his intestines
irradiate him with dragon's breath
introduce demons into his livers and spleen.

At night Sir Galahad weeps.
Tears stain his tunic.
His life drips into the bag at his side.

Prognosis

The patient talks to the consultant of Oxbridge colleges, London clubs. They are at ease, men of a different world from that of the other patients in this urology ward. Without shifting gear the consultant tells him that he has cancer of the liver and that it's heading to his heart. The patient considers this information, opts for chemo as if he were choosing the crème brulée.

Dogfight

Phil is cleared for take off:
the runway of the ward rumbles –
he waves from the cockpit of his bed,
oxygen mask distorting the face
of a man on a solo mission.

Touchdown is the single bed ward.

He flies on morphine waves;
rolling, bucking and groaning,
lost in this last dogfight,
turbulence rocking his body.

Tonight down the corridor in free fall
Phil's voice full of fear and madness

then the door will shut.

To let

Now in recovery,
post-operative:
is this as good
as it's going to get?

I walk down her street
in wind-blown early spring.

Sign blue-tacked
to a window –
Flat To Let.

Sea-food

Dr Zhang and I
face each other over
a glass counter in the
Chinese Medicine Shop.

There is a translator on the phone
who could be in Beijing,

We pass the receiver back and fore
each question is framed, translated, answered:

> *Where is the prostate?*
> *How strong is your election?*
> *Do you feel acupuncture?*

The jars of ancient remedies offer no opinion.

I ask the translator

> *What brought the professor*
> *From Shandong University*
> *To Glebe Street, Penarth*
> *with no English, only*
> *remedies, roots and needles?*

Dr Zhang smiles
offers *King – male tonic pills.*
The translator says
Goodbye, and do not eat sea-food.

I drove 200 miles to read

to ten people in Penmachno

now I'm driving home
chasing my headlights

through floods
at Dolwyddelan

traffic lights
in the middle of nowhere

the fox crossing
near Blaenau Ffestiniog

under the swoop of an owl
luminous at Trawsfynydd

the bright light box
urinal at Mallwyd

past the hulk of the chapel
moored at Carno

racing the boy racer
from Llangurig to Rhayader

seeing RS Thomas' face
in the bend at Cwmbach

hearing my mother
pulling out of Builth

shouting *yma eto*
at Bronllys

my heart stopping
dropping past Pen-y fan

(once I hit a sheep here
its ghost still haunts me)

Merthyr doesn't exist anymore
the snow just melted

Cardiff's hellhole glow
waits and waits.

The business of bone

The shadows of clouds look like
a medieval map of the world
projected by autumn sun
onto the escarpment of Pen y fan.

Even to the whale
that spouts a white plume
of scattered sheep into the green yonder,
a moving mass of misplaced forestry.

I guess an observer there,
looking across at us, could
have the same thought; we
sift space between shifting continents.

Our business is bone
and healing after the accident
that cracked her vertebra like a cold twig
on this snow-covered slope.

We cannot decide where the sledge
catapulted her into casualty
and a New Years Eve on Ward 1
throwing up as fireworks spattered the windows.

Consigned to her hard carapace
through the unbending months of winter
in her whale-boned corsetry
she cut a dash in Sainsburys.

She is picking through other bones.
In a nest of wool a sheep's skeleton
arranges itself haphazardly –
it too the victim of chance disaster

skull broken, unzipped fragments,
only the teeth solid in their sockets
gritted in a grin against this wind
which shears the slope.

She studies these remains
counting vertebrae, beads
of a broken rosary –
through it all she kept the faith.

She looks away and down
at the bikers, bright as dragonflies,
burning up the mountain road.
The wind blows, the world changes.

New Year's Eve

I left you in your bed
and still haven't found my way.

The woman next to you
transfixed by the portable TV.

The woman opposite, howling –
she would last little longer than the year

which even now, as I walk through
empty corridors, tilts into oblivion.

Then out though the wrong door.
There are stars but no moon –

a nurse stands in the cold
smoking her last cigarette.

A rocket explodes, and I want
to see any face but that of the security man

who stamps his feet,
coughs and spits.

Caroline Street

The divide:
Brewery Quarter –
a brash 1/4 quarter
kitted out
in building designer gear
glossed in structural glass.
Quant orange rendered panels,
windows eyelined in grey steel,
balconies jutting
like a young slapper's tits:
hey – signature architecture.

This lot looks down on the
south side –
Dorothy's chip shop,
Tony's kebab, the burger bars –
feeling the sharp elbows
of the pushiest tart in town.

> (*Wasn't old man brewery
> carted off because the smell of hops
> clinging to his coat blistered
> Chanel like paint stripper?*)

In the day they skulk, shuffle feet
on cracked paving stones,
it's the daylight – it burns their eyes.

Come Saturday midnight
a tide roars through
strait Caroline.
The old fast food joints
throw chips, gristle and grease
into the gullets of the good timers;
a flotsam tide of food wrapping
slops and swirls ankle deep.
Lads on the lash piss
on the Brewery Quarter wall –
hell, they know which side of the street
their bread is buttered.
On to Life, Oz, Oxygen, Zync.
Glowing in the night
shin-kicking Caroline Street.

My funeral

I'm not so chipper now
back here for the post-op three-month check-up
with the grey-haired men clutching their wives
and papier mâché urine bottles.

The feedback from the GP's
blood test is not good.
Sister Vivienne is
putting a brave face on it.

Only this morning Robert De Niro
was thanking the world
for the success of his treatment –
Bob's kept me company.

Now he's out of the woods
and I'm in suite 18 contemplating
a PSA level that is too high and
rides on trolleys down corridors.

I'm already planning my funeral.
A pair of black stallions with plaited manes
will pull me Kray-like up Thornhill.
The rattle of those big wheels

will draw the crowds, children will see their faces
reflected in the lacquer of my casket.
There will be recordings of Bob Cobbing
and clips of De Niro saying *you talking to me?*

At the moment of cremation a butterfly will appear from
                                             nowhere.
The congregation will be stunned into silence.
Someone will whisper – *his nightmare is over now.*
Everyone will hear and nod – *yes, it could have been me*
                              (*but thank God it's him*)

Two days later the phone rings –
been a mistake, samples mixed up.
I sigh, get onto the crem
tell them to cancel the arrangements

or at least
put them on hold.

Appointment

Collisions of fingertips,
a thunderstorm of expectation in each glance:
the decoding, deciphering of the smallest gesture,
tectonic plates shifting
under the weight of her words.

She knows my body
in a way that few do.
Once, when I awoke,
she was there.

Now as we sit across the table
I'm bored, impatient,

the functional chairs,
bare table top,
vacant stares.

More bones

On the bus to the ossuary
I ask her whether it would be better
to lose my knob or a leg.

She replies leg.

Later we stare at a baroquery of bones,
bell-shaped piles, crenulations, chandeliers,
skulls slung like Christmas decorations.

Calcium lasts longer –
she pats a polished cranium –
but flesh is more fun.